WELCOME TO
SAMANTHA'S WORLD ❦ 1904
Growing Up in America's New Century

THE AMERICAN GIRLS COLLECTION

American Girl

Printed in Singapore
99 00 01 02 03 04 05 TWP 10 9 8 7 6 5 4 3 2 1
The American Girls Collection® and the American Girl logo
are trademarks of Pleasant Company.

Written by Catherine Gourley
Edited by Jodi Evert and Michelle Jones
Historical and Editorial Consulting by American Historical Publications
Designed and Art Directed by Mengwan Lin, Laura Moberly, Kimberly Strother, and Jane S.Varda
Produced by Mary Cudnohfsky, Cheryll Mellenthin, and Paula Moon
Cover Illustration by Dan Andreasen
Interior Illustrations by Chris Duke, Laszlo Kubinyi, Susan McAliley, and Jean-Paul Tibbles
Researched by Kathy Borkowski, Mary Davison, Maxine Fleckner Ducey,
Sally Jacobs, Ruta Saliklis, and Sally Wood
Prop Research and Styling by Jean doPico
Photography by Dan Dennehy, Connie Russell, and Jamie Young

Special thanks to the Lower East Side Tenement Museum
and the Museum of the City of New York

Library of Congress Cataloging-in-Publication Data
Gourley, Catherine, 1950-
Welcome to Samantha's world, 1904 — growing up in America's new century /
[written by Catherine Gourley ; edited by Jodi Evert and Michelle Jones].
p. cm. — (The American girls collection)
Summary: An in-depth look at life for girls and women in America in 1904, discussing
city and town life, social reform, new inventions, amusements, and more.
ISBN 1-56247-772-2
1. United States—Social life and customs—1865-1918—Juvenile literature. 2. United States—
Social conditions—1865-1918—Juvenile literature. 3. Girls—United States—Social life and
customs—Juvenile literature. 4. Girls—United States—Social conditions—Juvenile literature.
5. Women—United States—Social life and customs—Juvenile literature.
6. Women—United States—Social conditions—Juvenile literature.
[1. United States—Social life and customs—1865-1918.]
I. Gourley, Catherine, 1950- II. Duke, Chris ill. III. Title. IV. Series.
E168.G7 1999 99-24423 973.91—dc21 CIP

Table of Contents

Welcome to Samantha's World

*Cornelia's voice was strong and firm as she went on.
"The time has come for all of us to speak out. We must
stand up for what we believe is right!" she said.
"We must make up our own minds. The time has come
to change the old ways. Women **must** vote!"*

—Happy Birthday, Samantha!

The whole world was changing, or so it seemed to Samantha Parkington. If she listened closely, she could hear the sounds of new inventions: telephones ringing, electric lights buzzing, and automobiles rumbling and clanking. In factories, machines produced goods more swiftly and cheaply than human hands ever could. Surely progress was good!

Grandmary wasn't so sure. She had got along just fine before machines and people filled her life with noise and shocking ideas, like a woman's right to vote. Who should Samantha agree with—Grandmary or Aunt Cornelia, who believed in changing the old ways?

Samantha Parkington is a fictional character. But the time and place of her story—America at the beginning of the twentieth century—was real. In fact, all the characters in Samantha's world are drawn from the memories, letters, and diaries of real girls and women. Some of these real people lived in fabulous mansions. Others lived in small towns or on farms. Still others lived and worked in dark, filthy *tenement*, or apartment, buildings in crowded cities. The machines and new ideas changed the lives of them all.

In this book, you will travel back in time and experience the changing world that Samantha knew. You will meet these real people and hear their true stories. The journey begins as most journeys do . . . with a map.

A Growing Country

In 1904, America was just entering a brand-new century. It was called an age of confidence. Many Americans believed that the new ways of traveling, communicating, and manufacturing were good for the country. They were confident that progress would improve their lives.

However, Nellie showed Samantha that progress did not improve everyone's life. Changes that meant better and easier lives for the middle and upper classes often meant hardships for poor people, especially immigrant families.

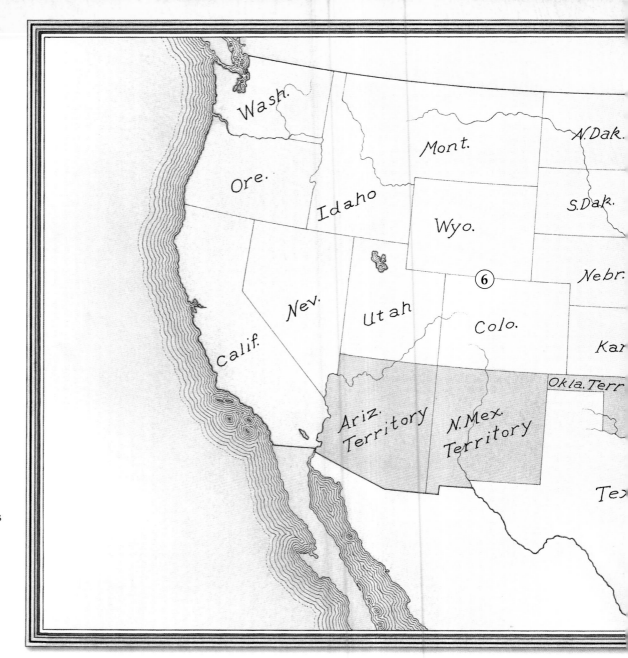

① IMMIGRANTS
Each week thousands of immigrants from Europe arrived at Ellis Island. Many of them did not speak English and had very little money. In the cities, they often lived in crowded tenement buildings.

② MILLIONAIRES
Wealthy families often lived in elegant mansions. In New York City, the homes built along Fifth Avenue were called "Millionaire's Row."

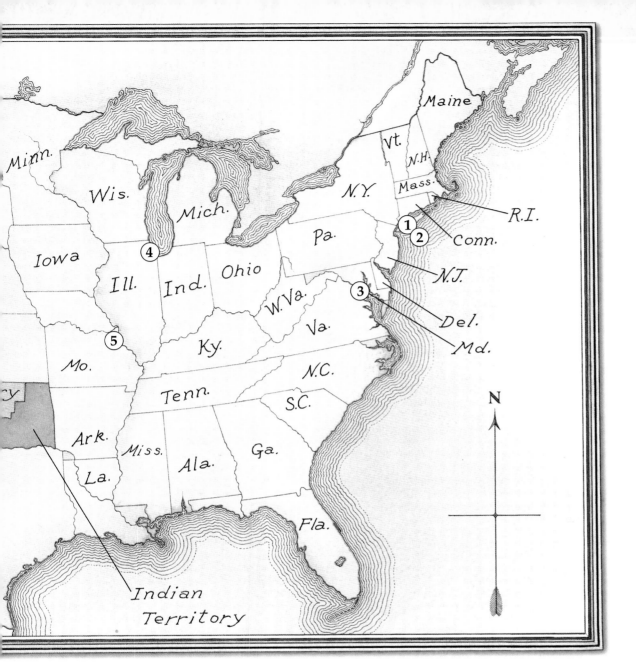

The map shows states including:
Maine, Vt., N.H., Mass., R.I., Conn., N.Y., Pa., N.J., Del., Md., W.Va., Va., Ohio, Ind., Ill., Mich., Wis., Minn., Iowa, Mo., Ky., Tenn., N.C., S.C., Ga., Ala., Miss., Ark., La., Fla., Indian Territory

N

⑥ OPPORTUNITY IN THE WEST

Trains carried immigrants and adventurers westward beyond the prairie of Kansas to work in the silver mines of Colorado, Wyoming, and Nevada. Many also went to California to pan for gold.

⑤ WORLD OF WONDERS

In 1904, more than 20 million visitors from around the world came to the World's Fair in St. Louis, Missouri, to see the latest inventions—including a display of one hundred different automobiles and the world's largest Ferris wheel.

③ A YOUNG LEADER

In 1901, 42-year-old Theodore Roosevelt was the youngest man to become president. Not everyone was confident that he could lead America into the new century.

④ WORKERS ON STRIKE!

Angry workers in factories, mills, and meatpacking plants walked off their jobs. They were on strike for more money, shorter workdays, and safer working conditions. Among the strikers were thousands of children.

3

Hustle-Bustle

In Samantha's time, America was a country on wheels. Trains rolled along thousands of miles of cross-country tracks, and automobiles rumbled down city streets. People were traveling farther and faster than ever before.

RIDING IN STYLE
For the wealthy, traveling across the country was a pleasurable pastime. Many enjoyed private railcars with pianos, brass beds, kitchens, and servants' quarters.

In New York City, steam locomotives ran on railroad tracks built above the sidewalks.

"Step lively," the trolley conductor told passengers. The trolleys were often jammed to the doors with riders.

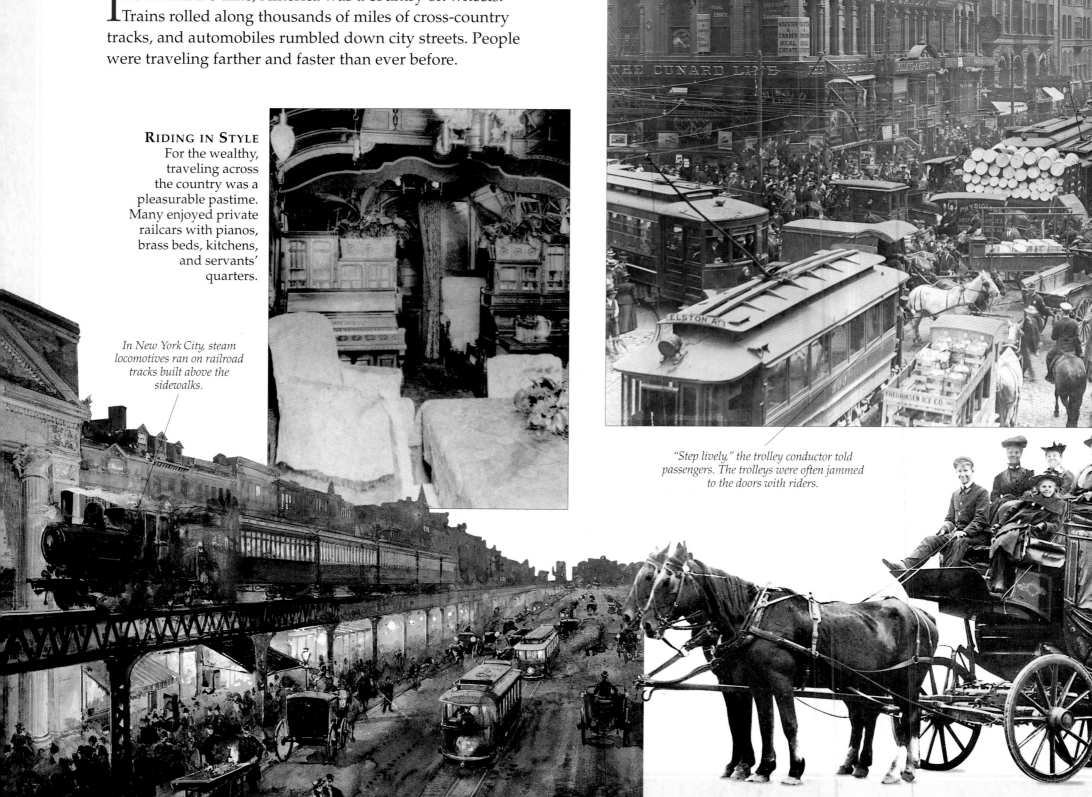

WINGS
In 1903, there were changes in the air, too. Orville Wright made the first successful flight aboard an aircraft. He glided across the sand dunes of Kitty Hawk, North Carolina.

TRAFFIC JAM
With so many trolleys, buses, automobiles, and horse-drawn wagons, city streets were almost impassable.

HONK!
Traveling by automobile was risky business. There weren't any traffic signals or stop signs yet, so drivers often ran into one another!

STAGECOACH
Railroad tracks didn't reach everywhere. In 1905, 23-year-old Ethel Waxman accepted a teaching position in the wilderness of Wyoming. The only way she could travel to the one-room schoolhouse was by old-fashioned stagecoach.

Going Down!

New York City needed a better way to move thousands of people from one part of the city to another. City leaders had already looked up and built elevated railroads. The only other direction to go was . . . down!

In 1900, the city began to dig a subway. Digging a tunnel for an underground train was backbreaking and dangerous work. More than 30,000 men—mostly Italian and Irish immigrants and African Americans—used pickaxes, shovels, and even explosives to dig the trenches for the new subway. For four years, they tunneled through solid bedrock, through quicksand bogs, under buildings, and even under rivers.

In October 1904, the city's newest form of transportation was ready for operation. More than 100,000 people—many dressed up in their very best clothes—gathered to "do the subway."

CHEWING GUM
The first chewing gum was tasteless balls of a plant sap called *chicle*. Soon gum was made into long, thin strips and flavors were added.

Newfangled Notions

Uncle Gard teased Grandmary that she had not kept up with modern times. By 1904, hundreds of new inventions had begun to change the way people lived, worked, and played.

SHOWERS
Some wealthy families had the newest convenience— a shower! Water sprayed in every direction from pipes that curled around the bather.

Lamps made by Tiffany and Co. often had glorious stained-glass shades.

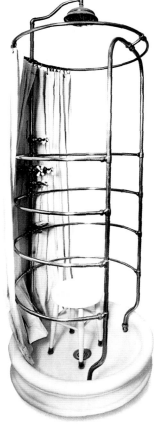

VRRROOOOM!
Women used to beat carpets with brooms to remove dust. In 1901, a new hand-pump machine lifted dirt from the rugs. Then, in 1908, William Hoover invented the motorized vacuum cleaner.

BRIGHT IDEA
In 1879, the electric lightbulb began to light up homes across the United States. Still, by the end of the century, fewer than ten percent of American homes had electricity.

TELEPHONES
Only some families had telephones in 1904. Several households shared the same telephone wires, called *party lines*. People often secretly listened to one another's calls.

In 1904, hot dogs cost five cents.

UP, UP, AND AWAY!
Steel *girders*, or supports, allowed builders to construct tall buildings called "skyscrapers." This skyscraper is called the Flatiron Building because it's shaped like the flat irons people used to press their clothes.

THE FIRST MOVIES
Buildings called *nickelodeons* had rows and rows of little movie machines. A person dropped a nickel into a machine, then turned the crank. The moving picture lasted about 15 seconds.

HOT DOG!
On the boardwalk on New York's Coney Island, Charles Feltman tried selling hot sausages wrapped in a roll. The public loved them! Soon, "hot dogs" were sold at snack stands and restaurants across the country.

PHONOGRAPHS
Phonographs let people listen to recorded music in their homes. A person simply turned the crank and placed the needle on the edge of the record. The large horn projected the sound.

Life in a Small Town

On a summer morning, a small-town girl might wake to the sound of a rooster crowing or a church bell ringing. Through her open window, she could smell freshly mowed grass and watch the neighbor's dog chase a rabbit across a field. Life in a small town was full of open spaces, fresh air, and friendly neighbors who stopped at the front gate to chat. But even in small towns, modern times had arrived.

① MANSIONS

The wealthy lived in mansions with large lawns and gardens. On a summer afternoon, families often played lawn tennis or croquet.

② FACTORIES

Inside the factory buildings, machines rumbled. Some machines stitched and sewed, while others pressed metal into things like can lids and bucket handles.

③ BOARDING HOUSES

Many factory workers were unmarried farm girls who lived in boarding houses. Sometimes two girls shared a single bed. Many of the girls sent their factory wages home to help their families.

④ LIBRARY

Most small towns had a library, where children spent hours reading the latest books—*Black Beauty*, *Alice in Wonderland*, or *The Secret Garden*.

11 MIDDLE-CLASS COTTAGES

Middle-class homes were small and plain. But in the summer, beautiful rosebushes climbed up trellises and filled the air with perfume.

10 CLOCK TOWER

A loud GONG! from the clock in the clock tower sounded the hour. Church bells also rang in the morning, at noon, and again in the evening.

8 DOCTOR'S OFFICE AND 9 HOSPITAL

The town doctor had an office in his home. Patients came without an appointment and waited until the doctor could see them. If they were very sick, the doctor sent them up the street to the hospital.

7 CHURCH

After a long day working in the factory, a young girl might walk to church for choir practice, to listen to a political speech, or to attend a church supper.

6 GAZEBO

On warm Sunday afternoons, families strolled through the park. They often stopped at the gazebo to listen to the band play.

5 TRAIN STATION

Passenger trains carried people to and from the small towns. Freight trains carried factory-made goods to larger cities, where they were sold.

Summer in the City

Like Samantha, Olga Marx was ten years old in 1904. She lived in New York City, where summer was a chorus of sounds and smells. Olga woke to the clip-clop of a horse pulling the dairy wagon. The milkman delivered fresh milk in a jug and left it with the cook who prepared all the meals in Olga's house. Next came the bakery wagon with fresh loaves of rye and wheat bread. Some mornings, Olga fed sugar cubes to the horses that pulled the delivery wagons.

A few blocks away, the rumblings of the elevated train, or the El, shook the windows of the city as men—and many women too—went to work. By noon the air was full of noise: the grinding wheels of carts and trolleys, the crack of drivers' whips over the backs of the workhorses, the shrill of a policeman's whistle. The ragman called out for old rags as he pushed his wheelbarrow through the crowds. "Any old clothes, any old clothes!"

The sun glared off the windows of the tall buildings crowded along the cobblestone streets. Wealthy men and poor men alike rolled up their sleeves to cool their wrists. Women carried parasols to shade their faces from the hot sun. Throughout the day, the pushcart vendors sold their wares—lemonade and ices, roasted peanuts and oranges. Other vendors hawked their services, crying "Knives to sharpen; scissors to grind!"

By evening, the sun had dipped behind the hot buildings. Overhead, the El still rattled. Sometimes Olga sat on the front steps of her house, waiting for the lamplighter to come. He stopped to light the gas lamps, one at a time.

Later, lying in her bed in the dark, Olga listened again to the clip-clop of horses. They were drawing *hansoms*, or covered carriages, now. The passengers inside these carriages were gentlemen and ladies going to the theater or to dine at garden restaurants on the city's rooftops. Then came the cries of the "newsies" selling the evening papers on street corners. "Extra! Extra!" the children's voices echoed into the night until they had sold their last paper.

By then, Olga was asleep.

Life in a Mansion

The sights and sounds of the city were different inside the mansions along Fifth Avenue, also known as "Millionaire's Row." The Fields were one of the families that lived there. Life for children in these mansions could be quite formal and strict. At exactly five o'clock each afternoon, Mrs. Field climbed the stairs to visit her children in the nursery. Sometimes she helped them do their homework or read to them. At exactly six o'clock, Mrs. Field went downstairs to dress for dinner or the opera. Her children did not see her again until the next day.

① Nurseries had bright colors, lots of toys, and child-sized tables and chairs.

NURSERY
Children's bedrooms and baths were on the top floor. They studied and ate most meals there. A live-in nurse, or *nanny*, took care of them.

② A **chaise** (shayz) longue, or fainting couch, was a good spot to rest when tight corsets made women dizzy.

BEDROOMS
Husbands and wives each had their own bedrooms and baths. Some women kept their jewels in safes hidden in their bedrooms.

Each night servants laid freshly starched nightclothes on the beds.

③ Furniture was arranged around a table for serving refreshments, close together to make conversation easier, and near the fire for warmth.

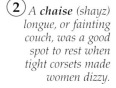

PARLOR
The lady of the house entertained guests in the parlor. The fancy furnishings showed the family's good taste.

④ The large mirror in the entrance hall, or **foyer**, was very expensive. It was a sign of wealth.

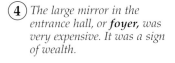

BALLROOM

After dinner, guests might be treated to music and dancing in the ballroom. During formal dances, an orchestra played graceful, elegant waltzes.

8 *A **parquet** (par-KAY), or patterned, wood floor was expensive, but perfect for dancing!*

DUMBWAITER

A small elevator called a *dumbwaiter* carried dishes from the kitchen to the dining room.

DINING ROOM

The lady of the house carefully planned the seating arrangements so each guest would have a pleasing and entertaining dinner partner.

7 *Under some dining tables, there was a button the lady of the house could press to call the butler.*

RECEPTION HALL

Guests were *received*, or greeted, in the grand reception hall, which was often two stories tall.

5 *As her guests arrived, the lady of the house made a dramatic entrance as she gracefully glided down the grand staircase.*

6 *In the basement, the servants worked in the kitchen preparing food. The lady of the house planned the meals, but she rarely cooked for her family.*

A Night at the Opera

When a society lady attended the opera, she might sit in a private box seat. Before the houselights dimmed, men and women peered through their opera glasses into the boxes of their neighbors and gossiped. Even after the curtain rose and the orchestra began to play, the spying and whispering continued. Music lovers often complained of the bad manners of the people who were more interested in one another than in the performers on the stage.

Libretto means "little book" in Italian. It tells the story of the opera.

PRICE 35 CENTS.

METROPOLITAN OPERA HOUSE
GRAND OPERA
GIULIO GATTI-CASAZZA
ANDREAS DIPPEL
LIBRETTO
THE ORIGINAL ITALIAN, FRENCH OR GERMAN LIBRETTO WITH A CORRECT ENGLISH TRANSLATION

TOSCA

PUBLISHED BY
F. RULLMAN.
111 BROADWAY, NEW YORK.
THEATRE TICKET OFFICE.
THE ONLY CORRECT AND AUTHORIZED EDITION.

GORGEOUS GOWNS
Women's elegant evening gowns were a show all by themselves. Satins and silks shimmered and glass beads gleamed under the houselights.

*A glittering **tiara** (tee-AR-uh), or tiny crown, and a stunning strand of jewels were the grand finale of a lady's opera attire.*

Ladies sparkled from head to toe!

Opera glasses for peering at performers . . . and the audience

Silk gloves covered most of a lady's arm and had as many as 20 tiny buttons.

THE DIVA
One of the most popular _divas_ (DEE-vuz), or opera stars, was Adelina Patti. She is dressed as Rosina in _The Barber of Seville,_ a popular comic opera.

After the performance, roses were given to the opera singers to congratulate them.

The Queen of Song

Adela Juana Maria Patti first began to sing when she was just seven years old growing up in New York City. All the very best divas were European, however, not American. So Adela changed her name to Adelina Patti, sailed to England, and soon became the most famous opera singer in the world. As she took her final bows, audiences threw mountains of flowers on the stage.

Adelina at age 10

In the autumn of 1882, she returned to America as "the Queen of Song." In Boston, she commanded five thousand dollars for a performance. When the theater manager said he had only four thousand to pay, she agreed to sing . . . but without her shoes! This was shocking for any lady, but more so for the greatest diva of all time.

That evening, Adelina Patti arrived backstage fully dressed, but her feet were bare. The manager quickly produced another eight hundred dollars. The diva smiled and slipped on one shoe. Just as the curtain was about to rise, the manager found another two hundred dollars. Adelina Patti stepped onstage— fully dressed—and sang until the audience wept.

Amusements

Small towns, too, had their opera houses. On these smaller stages, traveling performers sang and danced and told jokes. If a town didn't have an opera house, the performers played wherever they could—in schools, churches, or town halls. Of course, not all amusements required a stage. A girl like Samantha could be the star of her own make-believe games, whether she was riding a painted carousel horse or taking an imaginary journey to a faraway land with a magic lantern show.

ANNIE OAKLEY
Open fields became theaters for traveling circuses and Wild West shows. Daredevils on horseback and sharpshooters like Annie Oakley were the stars of these shows.

ESCAPE ARTIST
Harry Houdini traveled from town to town thrilling audiences with his daring escapes from cuffs, chains, and containers like milk cans and bank vaults.

CAROUSEL
As the painted ponies turned, riders reached out and tried to catch a small brass ring. If they caught it, they won a free ride.

BALLROOM

After dinner, guests might be treated to music and dancing in the ball-room. During formal dances, an orchestra played graceful, elegant waltzes.

8 *A* ***parquet*** *(par-KAY), or patterned, wood floor was expensive, but perfect for dancing!*

DUMBWAITER

A small elevator called a *dumbwaiter* carried dishes from the kitchen to the dining room.

DINING ROOM

The lady of the house carefully planned the seating arrangements so each guest would have a pleasing and entertaining dinner partner.

7 *Under some dining tables, there was a button the lady of the house could press to call the butler.*

RECEPTION HALL

Guests were *received*, or greeted, in the grand reception hall, which was often two stories tall.

5 *As her guests arrived, the lady of the house made a dramatic entrance as she gracefully glided down the grand staircase.*

6 *In the basement, the servants worked in the kitchen preparing food. The lady of the house planned the meals, but she rarely cooked for her family.*

13

A Night at the Opera

When a society lady attended the opera, she might sit in a private box seat. Before the houselights dimmed, men and women peered through their opera glasses into the boxes of their neighbors and gossiped. Even after the curtain rose and the orchestra began to play, the spying and whispering continued. Music lovers often complained of the bad manners of the people who were more interested in one another than in the performers on the stage.

Libretto means "little book" in Italian. It tells the story of the opera.

PRICE 35 CENTS.

METROPOLITAN OPERA HOUSE
GRAND OPERA
GIULIO GATTI-CASAZZA
ANDREAS DIPPEL

LIBRETTO
THE ORIGINAL ITALIAN, FRENCH OR GERMAN LIBRETTO WITH A CORRECT ENGLISH TRANSLATION.

TOSCA

PUBLISHED BY
F. RULLMAN.

111 BROADWAY, NEW YORK.
THEATRE TICKET OFFICE
TRINITY BUILDING (BROAD ARCADE)
THE ONLY CORRECT AND AUTHORIZED EDITION.

GORGEOUS GOWNS
Women's elegant evening gowns were a show all by themselves. Satins and silks shimmered and glass beads gleamed under the houselights.

*A glittering **tiara** (tee-AR-uh), or tiny crown, and a stunning strand of jewels were the grand finale of a lady's opera attire.*

Ladies sparkled from head to toe!

MAGIC LANTERNS
Magic lanterns were early slide projectors. The gaslight inside the lantern projected the image on a wall.

Glass slides showed viewers faraway places—like the frozen land of Norway.

ROLLER-SKATING
Almost every city and town had its own indoor roller rink. At the most fashionable rinks, skaters glided to the music of a live band.

TEDDY BEAR
The teddy bear was named for President "Teddy" Roosevelt after he refused to shoot a bear cub on a hunting trip.

PHOTOGRAPHY
In 1900, Kodak Company produced the "Brownie," the first camera made especially for children. It cost one dollar. For the first time, many children could take snapshots of family and friends.

BLUB-BLUB-BUBBLES
A little soap in a bowl of water gave children hours of fun. They blew bubbles through a straw or a bubble pipe.

PING-PONG
Some families played Ping-Pong, an indoor version of lawn tennis, on their dining room tables. Some people played it so much they developed an ailment doctors called "Ping-Pong ankle"!

Bicycles and Bloomers

At the turn of the century, many new sports and games were open to women for the first time. With these new sports came new ideas about fashion. Until then, girls and women only wore skirts and dresses. Then fitness-minded girls and women began wearing *bloomers*, or full pants gathered at the knee. One writer even urged ladies everywhere to "Undo your corset ties and breathe!" Such talk would have shocked Grandmary!

GYMNASTICS
Gymnasts wore *gym slips*, or tunics and bloomers, so it was easier to run, jump, and hang from rings.

BICYCLING
Bicycling was all the rage in 1904. It even created a new fashion—the split skirt. The skirts allowed more freedom of movement but also showed a shocking bit of a lady's booted ankle!

Tennis rackets with "fishtail" handles were the height of fashion.

The lacing on the chain guard helped keep skirts from getting caught.

LAWN TENNIS

Upper-class women still dressed elegantly for an afternoon of lawn tennis.

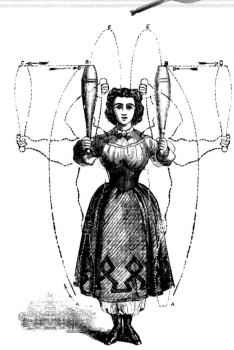

CLUBS

Women and girls used clubs to do exercises that helped them become stronger and more graceful. There were so many different moves that each move was labeled with a letter of the alphabet.

Imagine playing field hockey in a long skirt and lace-up boots!

BASKETBALL

The first women's college basketball game was played at Smith College in 1893. Soon after, the sport became popular with girls everywhere. At that time, people tossed balls into baskets on tall poles instead of through hoops.

Sometimes bathing dresses became so waterlogged girls held on to ropes so they wouldn't be carried away by the tide.

BATHING DRESSES

Bathing dresses were made from a type of silky wool called *alpaca*. Underneath, a woman wore drawers, silk stockings, and bathing slippers.

Clean and Presentable

The ideas about exercise were new, but people had long believed that "cleanliness is next to godliness." Many people, like Samantha and Grandmary, still bathed in the privacy of their own bedrooms. They had a *commode*, or washstand, with a washbowl and pitcher. Each day, they washed with cold water because they believed it was healthier than hot water.

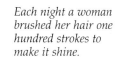

A SOOTHING SOAK
Some homes had bathtubs, but most didn't have running water in 1904. Servants filled the tub bucket by bucket. This woman is adding soothing bath salts to her bathwater.

SHAMPOOS
People washed their hair with bar soap, bottled hair washes, and even eggs. Twice a month, a woman came to Olga Marx's house to give her an egg shampoo. "I can still feel the little thud and that gooey feeling," remembered Olga.

Women put cold cream on their faces and hands to soothe their skin.

Each night a woman brushed her hair one hundred strokes to make it shine.

A LADY'S DRESSING TABLE
A proper lady had a dressing table full of everything she needed for her daily beauty routine.

A woman used a mirror to check the back of her upswept hairdo.

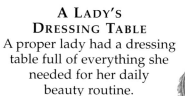

Pretty hair combs kept a woman's long hair in place.

CURLS
The wick on the curling iron stand was soaked in oil, then lit. The flame heated the curling iron rod.

Wick

SWEET SMELLS
Each morning, a lady took the glass stopper from one of her perfume bottles and dabbed a dot behind each ear.

*Some women used powder and **rouge** (rooj), or blush, so they would have a "healthy glow."*

The Wash Week

Keeping clothes presentable was hard work. Many housewives hired a wash girl like Nellie. Ladies' magazines recommended dividing wash tasks into the days of the week.

On Monday, the wash girl *steeped*, or soaked, the clothes to loosen the dirt. Tuesday was wash day. The wash girl soaped the clothes and scrubbed them on a washboard. Then she laid them in a second tub, poured boiling water over them, and let them soak for 30 minutes. Next, she drained the clothes, rinsed them with clean water, and hung them out to dry. On Wednesday, she dipped the cuffs, collars, and shirts in starch. Thursday was ironing day. The wash girl heated her irons on the stove. On Friday, she aired the clothes so they would smell fresh. At last, on Saturday, the wash girl carried the clothes and bedding to the rooms. But she couldn't rest for long. Soon it would be time to start the wash week all over again!

Monday

Tuesday

Wednesday

Thursday

Friday

Saturday

The Road to Good Health

People's growing interest in exercise as a road to good health triggered all kinds of new health care products and foods. New medicines like aspirin and the discovery that germs spread diseases made Samantha's world a safer and healthier place to live.

A HEALTHIER START

In Samantha's time, many families ate breakfast foods like bacon and sausage every morning. Dr. John Harvey Kellogg and his brother William experimented with cereals, which they said were much healthier than meat for breakfast. But not everyone liked these new health foods. They called them "shredded doormats," "gripe nuts," or "eata-heapa-hay"!

One thing you won't find inside this medicine chest is vitamins. They hadn't been discovered yet!

Be Fair to the Little Folks —They Are Worth It

IN most homes "nothing is too good for the children," and the little folks enjoy the tender crispness and delicate flavor of Kellogg's — the Original Toasted Corn Flakes.

In other homes the motto is "anything will do for the children"—even the tough, tasteless imitations of Kellogg's.

KRUMBLES is Kellogg's all-wheat food. Every single tiny shred is thoroughly toasted.

W. K. Kellogg

Kellogg's TOASTED CORN FLAKES

COCA-COLA
The makers of Coca-Cola first advertised the drink as a cure for upset stomachs. By 1903, drugstores sold Coca-Cola as a delicious and refreshing soft drink.

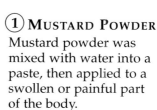

① MUSTARD POWDER
Mustard powder was mixed with water into a paste, then applied to a swollen or painful part of the body.

② SARSAPARILLA
Ads claimed sarsaparilla helped *purify*, or clean, people's blood. It tasted like root beer.

⑧ Aspirin

People had long used willow bark to ease pain, but in 1897, a chemist found a way to make a similar medicine in his lab. He called it *aspirin*.

⑦ Antiseptic

Cleaning wounds to prevent infections was a new idea for a new century.

⑥ Castor Oil

Many parents gave their children weekly doses of castor oil as a cure for everything that ailed them. It was thick like vegetable oil, and it tasted terrible!

⑤ Talcum Powder

This mineral helped absorb odors and perfumed and softened the skin.

③ Foot Powder

Feet cramped into tight-fitting shoes all day could produce as much as a full glass of sweat! Foot powder cooled the skin and absorbed perspiration.

④ Tooth Powder

People brushed their teeth with tooth powder and water.

Vaccines were created to help the body fight off germs.

Microscopes helped doctors discover new germs.

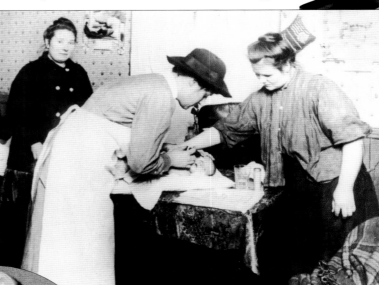

Germs

Doctors were just beginning to understand that germs spread disease. Surgeons started washing their hands before and after an operation, and they no longer used the same operating knife on more than one patient without first cleaning it!

Visiting nurses went to tenements to help heal the sick and teach mothers how to prevent diseases.

A Future President

As a child, Theodore Roosevelt suffered from asthma. As a young man, he exercised hard to build up his body's strength. When he became a father, he encouraged his children to climb, run, and swim as hard and as far as they could.

Meet the Roosevelts

When Theodore Roosevelt became president in 1901, he and his family—including six young children—moved into the White House. The president had two strict rules: the children could not go downstairs during public visiting hours or interrupt the president while he was at work. Upstairs, however, life in the White House was rough-and-tumble. Often the president sneaked up the steps for a game of Hide-and-Seek. The family's laughter could be heard throughout the hallways!

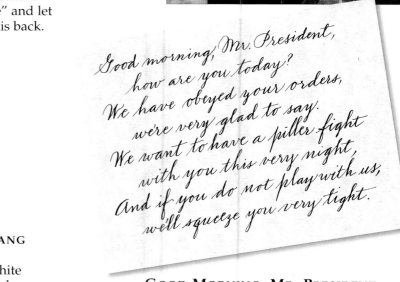

Quentin, President Roosevelt, Theodore Jr., Archie, Alice, Kermit, Mrs. Roosevelt, and Ethel in 1903

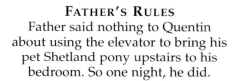

FATHER'S RULES
Father said nothing to Quentin about using the elevator to bring his pet Shetland pony upstairs to his bedroom. So one night, he did.

WHITE HOUSE FUN
The president's children walked on stilts, roller-skated, and sometimes used the sofas as trampolines. Often the president played "horse" and let them ride on his back.

THE WHITE HOUSE GANG
Quentin and Archie, who called themselves "the White House gang," played pranks on the Secret Service men. They dropped water balloons over balcony railings and jumped out of cabinets.

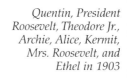

Good morning, Mr. President, how are you today? We have obeyed your orders, we're very glad to say. We want to have a piller fight with you this very night, And if you do not play with us, we'll squeeze you very tight.

GOOD MORNING, MR. PRESIDENT . . .
The Roosevelt children left notes for their father around the White House.

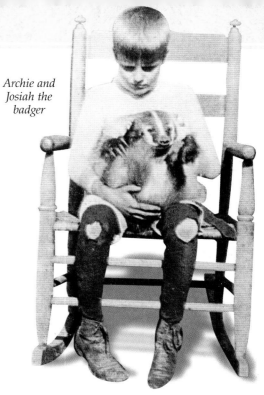

Archie and Josiah the badger

T.R., as the president was called, wrote this story for one of his sons. He even drew the pictures!

THE WHITE HOUSE PETS

All of the Roosevelt children had pets in the White House. They included a badger, a lizard, a mouse, a parrot, and even a small black bear! Loretta the parrot often squawked, "Hooray for Roosevelt!"

VACATION GAMES

On vacation, the president sometimes made up games, like the point-to-point walk. The children had to travel from one place to another in a straight line. That meant climbing a tree or swimming across a creek if it was in the way.

ALICE

Alice would soon be a *debutante* (DEB-yoo-tahnt) and hold her "coming out" society ball in the White House. But she was also known to join her brothers and sisters in sliding down the stairs on large silver serving platters.

Alice as a debutante in 1902

Meet the Gilbreths

Frank and Lillian Gilbreth were *efficiency experts.* They studied human motion in an attempt to discover the one best way of performing any task. Factory owners hired them to find the best way for people to do their jobs.

The aim of life is happiness, Frank and Lillian believed. The way to have more "happiness minutes" was to stop wasting time on unimportant tasks. Even at home, Frank and Lillian insisted that their 12 children find the one best way to do everything—from brushing their teeth to getting dressed in the morning! In the Gilbreth home, Father's stopwatch was always clicking on and off.

COLLECTIONS
Lillian encouraged her children to keep collections of such things as stamps, arrowheads, and dolls. Collections were a good use of time because they were both fun and educational.

ONE BEST WAY
"There is one best way of doing anything—whether it's building an automobile, eating an apple, or raising a family," Father said. In the Gilbreth house, spelling bees, math quizzes, even listening to the radio were family affairs.

MORNING ASSEMBLY
When Father returned from a business trip, he whistled to call the family to assemble. One morning, it took 18 seconds. His thumb clicked on the stopwatch. "Not bad," he said. "I still say we should make it in less."

FRENCH LESSONS
Both the boys and the girls had phonographs in their bathrooms. While the children brushed their teeth, they listened to French language records.

ANNE'S DATE

By the 1920s, the oldest Gilbreth daughter was going to her first prom. Anne cut her hair into a bob without Father's permission. He was upset until she convinced him it was more efficient. It took only 15 seconds to comb!

SHAVING TIME

One time Father even tried shaving with two razors. And he always buttoned his vest from the bottom up—rather than from the top down—because it saved him 40 seconds!

OPEN WIDE!

One year, six children— plus Father—had their tonsils removed. Father hired a photographer to make a movie of the physician's movements. All day, the poor photographer stood in the makeshift operating room in the parlor, fighting the thick fumes of *ether* (EE-ther), a drug used to put patients to sleep.

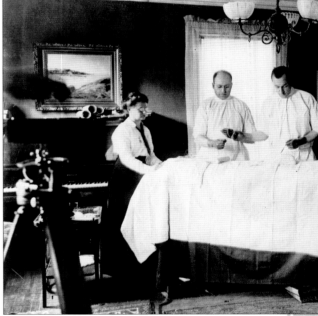

FOOLISH CARRIAGE

The family's automobile saved precious travel time. The children called it the "foolish carriage." Father steered it down the middle of the road, blowing the horn to warn other cars— and people, too!—to get out of his way.

27

The Shop Window

Store owner L. Frank Baum made "happiness moments" by creating magical displays for his shop windows. People walking by stopped and stared at the mechanical gadgets he had built—Ferris wheels that turned, stars that twinkled, and butterflies that fluttered. "People will always stop and stare at something that moves," said L. Frank Baum. He was right. By 1904, middle- and upper-class Americans had more leisure time and had discovered the pleasure of window-shopping—and buying!

From the book Samantha's Surprise

Girls like Samantha gazed at the toys in the shop window and dreamed.

THE WIZARD OF OZ
L. Frank Baum wrote this American fairy tale in 1899. The idea for the character of the Tin Man came from one of his store window displays.

FLEXIBLE FLYER
Both girls and boys sped down the slopes on this popular new sled.

FAIR PLAY
Now that many people had more leisure time, they were able to go to fairs and amusement parks. The new, exciting rides inspired toys like this mechanical Ferris wheel.

GIDDYAP AND GO!
Americans shopped for toys more than ever before, and factories stepped up production to meet the demand. Large toys, like rocking horses, also came from the factory as ready-to-build kits.

DOLLHOUSES

Girls spent happiness hours—not just minutes—playing make-believe in the many rooms of their dollhouses.

The first box of Crayola crayons was sold in 1903.

PRETTY PACKAGES

This cooking set had everything from cabinets to a coffee grinder arranged attractively in one easy-to-purchase package.

FRENCH BÉBÉS

Fancy toy stores carried French *bébés* (BAY-bayz), or child dolls. This doll was 36 inches tall, as tall as a small girl! She came with a dress for each day of the week, matching bonnets and shoes, purses, jewelry, and a hairbrush.

Dressing Up

Just like the fashion dolls, wealthy girls and women had many dresses to choose from. A proper woman like Grandmary might have changed her outfit four or five times a day, depending upon her social schedule!

At the turn of the century, girls and women began shopping in the new large department stores. When they strolled by the windows, they saw the latest styles for every social occasion: morning walks, afternoon teas, and evening dinners.

PLAY PINAFORES
Girls were expected to keep their dresses neat and tidy, so they wore *pinafores*, or aprons, when they played.

This fancy dress is the same style as a play dress, but it's made of finer fabrics—silk, velvet, and lace.

Sailor suits and middy dresses were popular in 1904. They often came with a whistle.

LOOSEN UP!
In 1904, children who didn't have to work had more time to play. Girls wore dresses with roomy *blouson* (BLOUS-on) tops and dropped waists, and boys started wearing *knickers*, or knee-length pants.

Even in the summer, girls and boys wore black cotton stockings and lace-up boots.

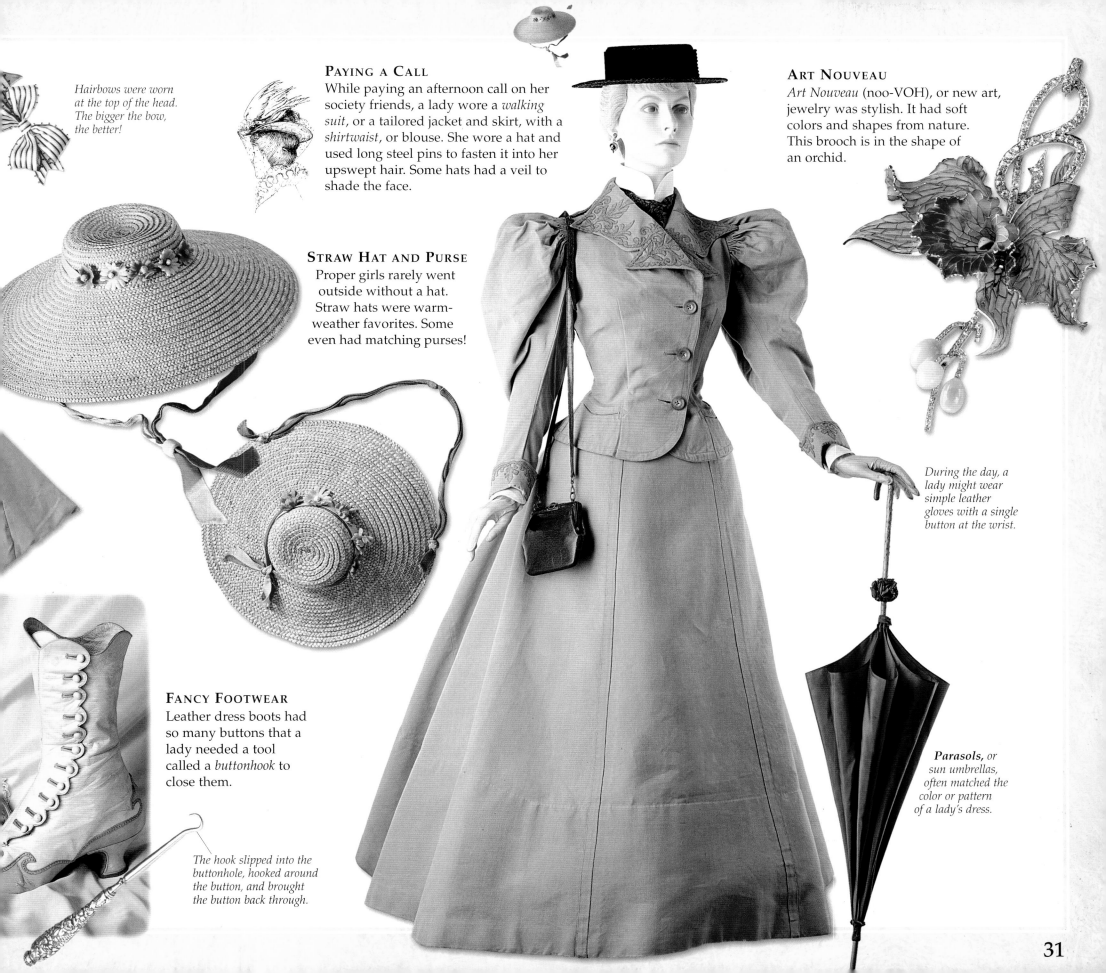

Hairbows were worn at the top of the head. The bigger the bow, the better!

PAYING A CALL

While paying an afternoon call on her society friends, a lady wore a *walking suit*, or a tailored jacket and skirt, with a *shirtwaist*, or blouse. She wore a hat and used long steel pins to fasten it into her upswept hair. Some hats had a veil to shade the face.

ART NOUVEAU

Art Nouveau (noo-VOH), or new art, jewelry was stylish. It had soft colors and shapes from nature. This brooch is in the shape of an orchid.

STRAW HAT AND PURSE

Proper girls rarely went outside without a hat. Straw hats were warm-weather favorites. Some even had matching purses!

During the day, a lady might wear simple leather gloves with a single button at the wrist.

FANCY FOOTWEAR

Leather dress boots had so many buttons that a lady needed a tool called a *buttonhook* to close them.

The hook slipped into the buttonhole, hooked around the button, and brought the button back through.

Parasols, *or sun umbrellas, often matched the color or pattern of a lady's dress.*

31

COURTING

Once young men and women had been introduced, they were permitted to *court*, or spend time together. They talked, played games, and even knitted together.

THE ENGAGEMENT

When a gentleman proposed and the lady and her parents accepted, he slipped a diamond ring onto the third finger of her left hand. This tradition followed the belief that a vein ran from that finger directly to the heart.

TOKENS OF LOVE

During courtship, couples exchanged tokens of love such as letters, locks of hair, rings, small portraits, and bouquets of daisies or violets.

An Invitation to a Wedding

In Samantha's time, a mother taught her daughter how to dress and how to behave properly so that she might attract a husband. A young lady might meet her future husband while attending church, the theater, or an evening ball. If a lady caught a gentleman's eye, the polite thing for the man to do was ask someone to introduce them formally. Then the gentleman might present his card to a lady, asking if he could escort her home. But the lady need not accept right away. She could wait to see what other cards she received and then decide which gentleman best suited her fancy. Even then, a lady never went anywhere alone with a gentleman without first seeking her mother's permission.

Before the wedding, a bride often hosted a lunch or dinner for her bridesmaids.

MARIA'S WEDDING DRESS
An immigrant bride like Maria Serafina Colonna wore a simpler wedding dress made of linen damask and lace. Fancier dresses were made of shimmering silk or satin and had long, flowing trains.

BRIDAL BOUQUET
In her bouquet, a bride carried orange blossoms, a symbol that the couple would have many children. It was the most popular flower for weddings.

Orange blossoms

Blue ribbons were for "something blue."

WEDDING CAKE
At some weddings, the cake was cut and packed in boxes tied with ribbon. As the guests left, they took a box of wedding cake as a souvenir.

BRIDAL TROUSSEAU
A society bride spent months shopping for her bridal *trousseau* (troo-SO), or outfit. She followed the saying "Something old, something new, something borrowed, something blue, and a silver sixpence in her shoe."

A society wedding might take months of planning, but the ceremony often lasted less than ten minutes!

A bride usually wore jewelry that was a gift from the groom. These pearls may have been a bride's "something new."

Made to Marry

Not every woman was in love with the man she married. This was true of Consuelo Vanderbilt's marriage.

On Consuelo's 18th birthday, dozens of red roses arrived at her family's mansion on Fifth Avenue. The card that came with the flowers had no name, but Consuelo knew who her admirer was—Winthrop Rutherford. They had secretly pledged their love and agreed to marry.

When Alva Vanderbilt discovered her daughter's secret love affair, she was determined to end it. The man Alva had selected to marry her daughter was the Duke of Marlborough. He was a British military hero and the holder of a royal title. Consuelo wept. She swore she would never marry the duke. "I don't ask you to think," Alva Vanderbilt told her daughter. "I do the thinking. You do as you are told."

This was to have been Consuelo's debutante year—a year of balls and skating parties, escorts and elegant dinners. She should have been filling the pages of her scrapbook with invitations, pressed flowers, and dance cards. Instead, Alva whisked her daughter away from society to Marble House, the Vanderbilts' summer mansion in Newport, Rhode Island. There Consuelo became a prisoner, never out of her mother's or governess's sight.

"Friends called but were told I was not at home," Consuelo said. "Locked behind those high walls . . . I had no chance of getting any word to Winthrop."

Alva took the letters Consuelo wrote and discarded those Winthrop had written to her. Meanwhile, Alva invited the duke to be her guest at Marble House. With his arrival, the social balls and dinners began again. But always, the duke was Consuelo's escort.

On a quiet evening that summer, the duke proposed. Earlier, a family doctor had told Consuelo that her mother had a bad heart and might suffer a heart attack if Consuelo disappointed her. Consuelo agreed to the marriage.

"I spent the morning of my wedding in tears and alone; no one came near me," Consuelo said. Her carriage arrived at St. Thomas Church 20 minutes late. Her eyes had been so swollen with tears that she had needed time to soothe them and calm herself. In those 20 minutes of waiting in the church, Alva feared her plans might have failed after all. And then the dutiful bride arrived.

At the altar Consuelo glanced shyly at her husband, but he did not look at her. He stared coldly ahead.

As the couple left the church, newspaper reporters crowded close for a glimpse of the bride and groom. Later, the duke confessed to Consuelo that he, too, had given up his true love to marry her. Their marriage was not one of love, but one of convenience—a wedding of British royalty and American money.

Making a House a Home

After a young woman married, she turned her attention to her new house. Magazines like *Ladies' Home Journal* published many practical tips to help a new housewife make her house a home. A "well-appointed home" was one that was always neat and clean. The young mistress had to have an eye for decorating with elegance without spending too much of her husband's money. She also had to have an even temper for managing her children and household help. That way her home would always be a peaceful place, the kind of place the magazines said a hard-working husband deserved.

Crazy quilts were patches of brightly colored scraps sewn together with flowers, animals, and initials embroidered on top.

SEWING

A woman's embroidery skills demonstrated her artistic talents and her ability to decorate her home without great expense. She made things like quilts, table covers, doilies, and pillows and displayed them in her parlor.

Needlework sewn on prepunched paper was inexpensive and easy.

Women often combined sewing techniques. This doily has crochet on the edges and both appliquéd and embroidered flowers.

Sewing boxes and tools were as beautiful and elaborate as a woman could afford. These tools are made from mother-of-pearl.

Books were filled with handicrafts, hobbies, and games especially for girls.

FLOWERS FOREVER
Girls and women pressed flowers from their gardens and from walks through the woods. Then they mounted them in frames and scrapbooks or on bookmarks.

PROPER PASTIMES
Well-to-do young girls spent their leisure time learning proper pastimes such as weaving, fancy needlework, painting, and flower arranging.

SCRAP SCREEN
The *decoupage* (day-koo-PAHJ) on this screen was a popular Victorian art. Women and girls pasted paper scraps onto furniture and coated them with a layer of varnish.

IN THE SHADE
Collecting flowers, shells, seeds, and butterflies showed a love of nature. Girls and women displayed their collections under glass domes called *shades*.

Time for Change

Ladies' magazines also warned women that men preferred charm and beauty to brains and independence. Even so, not all women gave up their dreams of an education or even a career. Hundreds of "lady doctors" and "lady lawyers" were at work across the country in 1904. Women were working in offices and newspapers and starting their own businesses. Many people had once believed that too much education could strain a woman mentally and weaken her physically. Those old-fashioned ideas were changing as one century ended and another began.

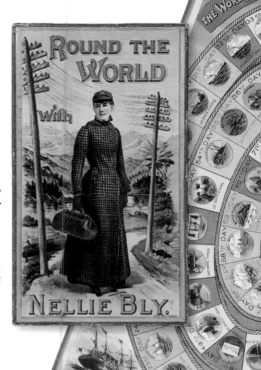

LADY REPORTER
Nellie Bly often disguised herself to go undercover to get a news story. For one assignment, she secretly entered a women's hospital for the insane to report on the harsh treatment of the patients.

SMILE!
Some women, especially journalists, became professional photographers. A woman named Frances Johnston was famous for her portraits of President Roosevelt and his family.

WATCHMAKER
Mamie Frey was one of the only woman watchmakers in Chicago. She was an expert, but some people still didn't trust a woman with their timepieces.

LADY DOCTORS
By 1910, six percent of the doctors in the country were women. Women learned about becoming doctors and nurses by observing them. Everyone in this class is a woman, even the patient!

Nellie performed another reporting stunt—traveling around the world in 72 days! A toy manufacturer created a board game about her amazing travels.

MADAM WALKER
Madam C. J. Walker created her own brand of hair-care ointments for African American women. Soon hundreds of women called "Walker Agents" were traveling door-to-door selling Madam's products. Madam Walker became America's first African American woman millionaire.

ISADORA DUNCAN
In 1898, Isadora Duncan performed her graceful "modern dance" for the first time. New York City audiences were shocked by her bare feet and flowing white robe. However, once she became a star in Europe, New York City changed its mind!

GOING TO COLLEGE
By 1900, more girls than boys were graduating from high school. Many continued their education in women's colleges or state universities that accepted both men and women.

Time to Vote!

Was it time for women to have the right to vote in political elections? People who believed yes, like Aunt Cornelia, were *suffragists*. People who thought no, like Grandmary, were *anti-suffragists*.

Suffragists fought hard to convince America that women should have the same voting rights as men. They marched through city streets carrying signs. They organized speeches in parks and in lecture halls. They knocked on door after door, asking men and women to sign petitions demanding that the government pass a new law giving women the right to vote.

Anti-suffragists argued that women would forget about their duties as wives and mothers if given the right to vote. Some feared that the *polling*, or voting, booths were unsafe places for women. Because people felt so strongly about women's voting rights, suffragist demonstrations were not always peaceful. Anti-suffragists sometimes shouted at marchers or threw rotten fruit at the speakers. Some suffragists were arrested for their demonstrations. But that didn't stop them. They were determined to change the law!

The Gift of Giving

ABBY ALDRICH ROCKEFELLER
When John D. Rockefeller Jr. asked his new wife, Abby, how she spent the large check he gave her as a wedding present, she replied, "I gave it away." That money went to the YWCA. Abby later built a hotel for working women, a community center for immigrant families, and New York's Museum of Modern Art.

At the turn of the century, a few very wealthy individuals were using their money to make the world a better place for all people. Instead of keeping all of their money for themselves, they gave away large amounts of it to worthy causes. This kind of gift giving is called *philanthropy* (fil-AN-thruh-pee), and the gift givers are *philanthropists*. They began a strong tradition of donating hundreds of thousands of dollars to build libraries, hospitals, museums, theaters, and public parks.

TODDLER PARKS
Fred Kirby and his wife used their money to build health clinics for poor children. In their hometown in Pennsylvania, the family also built a toddler park and play area. Nurses fed infants fresh goat's milk and cared for the children.

THE GIFT OF LEARNING
Andrew Carnegie built libraries in cities across America. He believed they encouraged people to improve their lives. Some of the libraries even had children's museums inside.

TIME IS MONEY

Banker J. P. Morgan hated to waste time. One busy day, Harvard Medical School officials asked him for money to expand the school. The banker glanced at his watch, then pointed to the building plans. He said, "I will build that, and that, and that. Good morning, gentlemen."

THE DIME GIVEAWAY

Billionaire John D. Rockefeller Sr. donated money for public buildings, but he also liked to surprise strangers he passed on the street by handing out shiny new dimes.

PARKS FOR THE PEOPLE

Many wealthy Americans gave land for public parks. William J. Gordon, a businessman in Cleveland, Ohio, built a city park with a bathing shelter on his lakefront property.

LADY BOUNTIFUL

People called Madam C. J. Walker "Lady Bountiful" for her contributions to African American orphanages, schools, and other charities. She said, "I love to use a part of what I make in helping others."

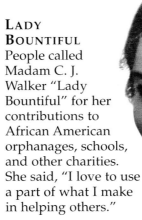

Freedom's Gift

A person didn't have to be wealthy to give money to a worthy cause. In France, thousands of ordinary citizens donated money to build a statue of liberty. They gave the statue to the United States to celebrate the friendship of the two countries and the ideal they shared that liberty and justice were for all. And once the statue arrived, it was ordinary Americans who contributed nickels, dimes, and dollars to build a pedestal so Lady Liberty could stand in New York Harbor. Newspaper publisher Joseph Pulitzer led the cause by promising to publish the name of anyone who donated money in his newspaper, *The New York World*.

Forever after, the lady became a symbol of freedom and hope for hundreds of thousands of immigrants. Many caught their first sight of her through a porthole window aboard a ship bound for Ellis Island.

Coming to America

Thousands of immigrants crowded onto ships. Sometimes there wasn't enough room to walk on deck.

For most immigrants, the Statue of Liberty was their first glimpse of America. Mothers lifted babies so they could see, too. The ship moved slowly past the statue and then dropped anchor near Ellis Island. Here immigration officials inspected all passengers and decided which were healthy enough to enter the United States. Each person on deck wondered, *Will America accept me, or will she send me back to my homeland?*

Main building

Ferry building

Main hospital building

ELLIS ISLAND

ARRIVAL
Small ferries shuttled immigrants from their ships to the main building. An American interpreter who spoke many languages led them up the stairs to begin their inspection.

Each passenger had a card with a number on it. The number told them which ferry to take to Ellis Island.

BAGGAGE
Immigrants had to leave their belongings in the baggage room while they went through inspection. When they returned, thieves might have stolen everything.

Doctors used a buttonhook to gently look under eyelids.

THE MEDICAL EXAM

Each immigrant had to have a medical exam. Immigrants who did not pass might go to the main hospital building. They could wait for hours or days to see if they would be allowed into America.

If a doctor found symptoms of a disease, he marked the immigrant with a piece of chalk. "E" was for an eye disease.

LANDING CARD

The next inspector asked questions like "How will you earn a living?" If the inspector was satisfied with the answers, he gave the immigrant a landing card. It was a ferry ticket to the mainland.

Red Star Line
Landing Card

Manifest Sheet No.

MAJESTIC

Name
Levenfish Miriam

List Number
2

MONEY EXCHANGE

Before immigrants left Ellis Island, they exchanged money from their homeland for American dollars.

Russian ruble note

German pfennig note

A NEW LIFE

When the ferry docked in New York Harbor, some immigrants went on to faraway cities. But many found rooms to rent in New York City.

CALIFORNIA
Cornucopia of the World

BOSTON
and New England Points
FROM NEW YORK

SHORE LINE
HARTFORD LINE
STONINGTON LINE
FALL RIVER LINE
PROVIDENCE LINE
NEW HAVEN LINE
BRIDGEPORT LINE
NORWICH LINE

GOVER

ad & Private Land F

Transfer Steamer Maryland Route from
WASHINGTON, BALTIMORE and PHILADELPHIA

Meet the Confinos

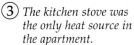

Victoria Confino and her family immigrated to America in 1913, after a terrible fire destroyed their beautiful home in Kastoria, Turkey. The family's new home was a tiny three-room *tenement* at 97 Orchard Street in New York City. Victoria missed her large home in Turkey with its gardens, fruit trees, and vineyards.

Like Samantha, Victoria loved school. In Mrs. Burck's second-grade class, she made A's and B's. But Victoria's father said she was needed at home to care for the younger children. So after her first year, Victoria sadly left school and stayed at home to help her family.

Families hung their ① clothing on wall pegs because tenement apartments had no closets.

The family brought some of ② their most precious belongings with them from Turkey, such as the lace bedspread and the family picture in the parlor.

③ The kitchen stove was the only heat source in the apartment.

DANCING LESSONS
Victoria loved to dance to the phonograph in the apartment. She taught her younger brother Turkish dances.

HELPING OUT
Most days Victoria helped cook the meals and scrub the floors. She rarely had time to do the things she loved, like playing or reading.

WHERE'S THE WATER?
The apartment had no running water. Victoria filled her bucket for cooking and washing from a pump in the hall. In the hall there were also two toilets that the Confinos shared with four other families.

⑤ *The Confino family celebrated the Sabbath on Friday at sundown. Mrs. Confino lit the candles and led the prayers.*

Some days Victoria helped at her father's clothing factory, pulling loose threads from shirts.

④ *A window between the living room and kitchen helped light pass through the apartment.*

A GOOD NIGHT'S SLEEP?
The Confino family of seven, plus two cousins, shared the three rooms in the apartment. The smaller children slept on chairs pushed together or on beds made from orange crates.

FAMILY TRADITIONS
The Confino family was Jewish. They kept alive their traditions in America. Each night Mr. Confino read the Yiddish newspaper. It read from right to left.

45

Behind Factory Walls

From the book *Samantha Learns a Lesson*

Many families, like Nellie's, were so poor that the children had to work and earn money to help the family survive.

N ellie shocked Samantha when she told her about the work she had done in a factory. At the turn of the century, many children worked in factories and mills across the United States. Children as young as three years old worked twelve-hour days, six days a week. They gave the money they earned to their mothers and fathers to help pay the rent or buy food.

THE COTTON MILL
Inside a cotton mill, the air was hot, humid, and dusty. The humidity kept the thin threads from breaking, but it was unhealthy for the children who worked there. Many became ill with lung diseases.

LONG, HARD DAYS
Factory managers hired girls to paste together artificial flowers for hat trims. The work was not difficult, but it was exhausting doing the same thing hour after hour, day after day.

At home, children did piecework such as cracking and shelling nuts for restaurants. Sometimes they cracked the hard shells with their teeth.

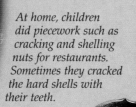

MAKING MOLASSES
In a molasses factory, girls filled jars and clamped lids on top. The hot, sticky syrup splattered on the girls as well as the floor and the nearby wall. Although the girls were careful, they still got burned.

THE WORKING LIFE
In mill villages, the factory whistle sounded before dawn. Children as young as six and seven tumbled out of bed for a breakfast of black coffee and biscuits. They worked from 5:30 A.M. to 7:30 P.M.

NIGHT SCHOOL
After working all day, some immigrant children went to night school to learn English. Many could not stay awake because they had worked so hard during the day.

The roar of the machines was so loud that a factory supervisor had to scream to be heard. If children talked, they could be fined.

The Triangle Shirtwaist Factory Fire

Pauline Pepe was 19 years old when she went to work in the Triangle Shirtwaist Factory in New York City. She worked on the eighth floor as a sewing machine operator and earned 12 dollars a week. She enjoyed her work and the friends she made. Some of the other workers were children much younger than Pauline.

The factory was not always a clean or safe place to work. Piles of clothing filled the aisles. The foremen often locked the factory doors to prevent the working girls from taking breaks or from stealing bits of ribbon and thread.

One Saturday afternoon, on March 25, 1911, just as Pauline and a friend were about to leave for the day, they heard the terrifying cry of "Fire!" The girls rushed for the doors, but they were locked. Within minutes, smoke filled the large room. Pauline lost sight of her friend. The girls pounded on the doors. They screamed, "Let us out! Open the doors!" The heat from the flames grew hotter. The mountains of clothing on the floor, on the tables, and in the work bins smoldered and then burst into flames.

Some of the girls rushed to the windows. Pauline heard the sound of breaking glass. She knew she would never have the courage to jump.

The girls were crying and coughing. They crowded against one another, pushing at the door. And then, at last, the door gave way. Someone had climbed the smoke-filled stairs to free the trapped workers.

A fireman guided them down the stairs. Outside, the street was a maze of confusion. Fire trucks blocked the streets, but their hoses didn't reach the sixth, seventh, and eighth floors where the fire was burning. Neither did the ladders. Many girls jumped, but most did not survive.

Pauline pushed through the crowd, looking for her friend. Was she one of the shattered bodies on the pavement? At last, Pauline found her. Like Pauline, her hair was burned and her coat tattered, but she was alive. They hugged each other and sobbed.

One hundred forty-six girls and women died in the fire. Some suffocated from the smoke as they huddled near the locked doors. *The New York Times* ran many stories of the fire and the investigation that followed. *Why were the doors locked?* the reporters asked.

The fire was a tragedy. Working men and women as well as society gentlemen and ladies demanded safer working conditions. Still, many years would pass before factories became safer places to work.

The Orphan Train

"They've picked me to go on the Orphan Train," Nellie said. "It's a train that goes out West, full of orphans from the city. The train stops in lots of little farm towns. People in the towns choose orphans to live with them and to work for them. Miss Frouchy says I have to go."
—Changes for Samantha

From the book *Changes for Samantha*

In large cities like New York, hundreds of children became orphans when one or both parents died from work accidents or disease. There were other kinds of orphans, too. They were children whose parents could not afford to feed or clothe them. These children wandered the streets, begging for food and sleeping in whatever shelter they could find. Some mothers who couldn't take care of their babies left them in the doorway of the New York Foundling Hospital.

A young minister named Charles Loring Brace began to raise money to send orphans by train to good homes away from the city. He gave each child a cardboard suitcase to hold their belongings—a pair of shoes, if they were lucky, and a change of clothes—and sent them west on orphan trains.

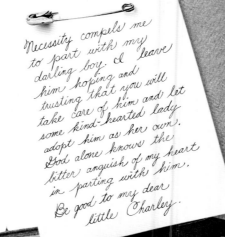

Necessity compels me to part with my darling boy. I leave him hoping and trusting that you will take care of him and let some kind-hearted lady adopt him as her own. God alone knows the bitter anguish of my heart in parting with him. Be good to my dear little Charley.

384

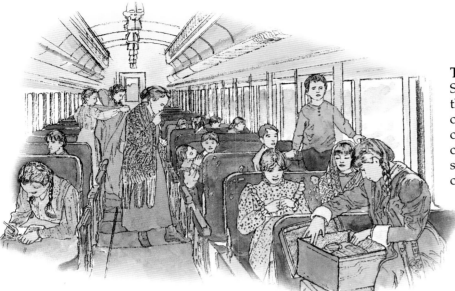

THE RIDE WEST
Several adults rode west with the children. They cared for the children and made sure they changed into their cleanest clothes when the train made a stop, so the children had the best chance of being adopted.

Words from the Orphan Train

Dear Mr. Brace,
When I lived in New York, I had no bonnet and now I have more bonnets than I can wear. And I get no whippings and I have a father and mother and brothers and sisters.

Ann

When a train made a stop, almost everyone in town came to see the children and to watch families choose their child.

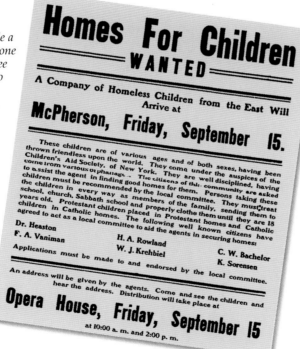

Homes For Children
WANTED

A Company of Homeless Children from the East Will Arrive at

McPherson, Friday, September 15.

These children are of various ages and of both sexes, having been thrown friendless upon the world. They come under the auspices of the Children's Aid Society, of New York. They are well disciplined, having come from various orphanages. The citizens of this community are asked to assist the agent in finding good homes for them. Persons taking these children must be recommended by the local committee. They must treat the children in every way as members of the family, sending them to school, church, Sabbath school and properly clothe them until they are 18 years old. Protestant children placed in Protestant homes and Catholic children in Catholic homes. The following well known citizens have agreed to act as a local committee to aid the agents in securing homes:

Dr. Heaston
F. A. Vaniman
H. A. Rowland
W. J. Krehbiel
C. W. Bachelor
K. Sorensen

Applications must be made to and endorsed by the local committee.

An address will be given by the agents. Come and see the children and hear the address. Distribution will take place at

Opera House, Friday, September 15
at 10:00 a. m. and 2:00 p. m.

The first day of school, I could hear whispers among the kids. "There's an orphan and he's going to be in our class..."
Elliott

ADOPTION
Farming families who needed extra workers for the fields often adopted orphans. Sometimes they took a brother but not his sister. Some orphans were treated well by their new families. Others weren't. Those orphans who didn't find a new home returned on the train to New York City.

Dear Friend,
The place where I lived I did not like. They whipped me till I was black and blue. I have a good place now. Please write to me with news of my mother.

Katie

In her own way, Samantha was a reformer. She helped Nellie and her sisters escape the cruelties of living in an orphanage.

From the book Changes for Samantha

The Reformers

The new century had many *reformers*, or people who worked to improve the quality of life for everyone. Some spent time in the tenement neighborhoods and alleys photographing and writing about what they saw. Others worked to improve safety in workplaces. Some reformers traveled across the country to speak in towns and cities about equal rights of all men, women, and children.

The tenement is a destroyer of house and character. A homeless city . . . is a despoiler of children, a destroyer of tomorrow.

— *Jacob Riis*

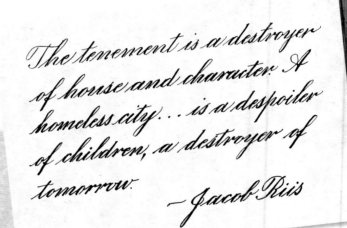

The photos and words of Jacob Riis helped convince city officials to improve housing for the poor.

HULL HOUSE
Jane Addams bought an old mansion in the Chicago slums and turned it into Hull House, a school, neighborhood center, and home for young working women. Mary Kenney O'Sullivan said one of the greatest moments of her life was coming to Hull House and discovering that people beyond the factory walls cared what happened to the workers.

In 1893, Hull House opened a music school with singing, dancing, and piano lessons for children.

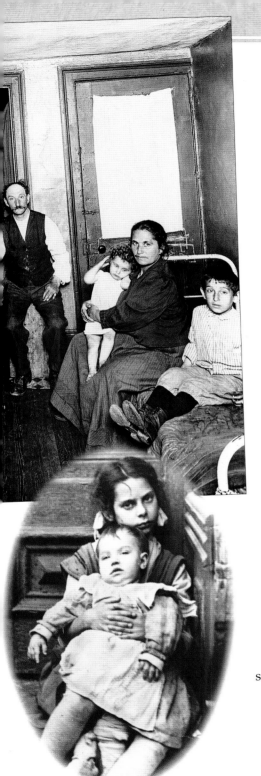

IDA B. WELLS
In some states, laws prevented African Americans from going to public places like parks and restaurants. Journalist Ida B. Wells wrote powerful stories to convince people to change unjust laws.

LYNCHING
Many black men were *lynched*, or killed by mobs, because people believed they had harmed white women. Ida B. Wells traveled across the country demanding new laws to protect *all* citizens.

LITTLE MOTHER
Jacob Riis photographed "little mothers"—girls who took care of their baby sisters and brothers while their parents worked.

PREVENTING CRUELTY
One day in New York City, Henry Bergh saw men beating an overworked horse. Soon after, Bergh founded the Society for the Prevention of Cruelty to Animals. Later, he worked to prevent cruelty to children, too.

This workhorse gets a cooldown on a New York street.

The March of the Mill Children

One of the most famous reformers of Samantha's time was a woman called Mother Jones. She devoted her life to helping all workers—in factories and mills, railroads and coal mines—earn better wages and have safer working conditions. She particularly wanted to help child laborers. Many had been injured by the factory machines.

On July 7, 1903, she led a march of children from Philadelphia all the way to President Roosevelt's summer home on Long Island— 125 miles away. By the time the parade reached New York City, newspapers were calling the protest "The March of the Mill Children."

Mother Jones

Thousands of Americans saw the children as they marched in the streets. Many more read about them in newspaper stories written by reporters who had followed the march from its start in Philadelphia. And that was just what Mother Jones had wanted—to make people more aware of the evils of child labor.

Saving Nature

Reformers worked to save nature, too. By 1904, railroads crisscrossed the country. Mining and logging camps spread into the western United States. The wilderness was disappearing, and reformers like John Muir wanted to save it.

He worked to preserve the Grand Canyon in northwestern Arizona and to save California's giant redwoods. These trees are "kings of the forest," he said. "Any fool can destroy trees. They cannot run away."

John Muir's words convinced President Roosevelt to set aside 148 million acres of forests. In 1908, Muir Woods in California was named in John Muir's honor. In that same year, the government made the Grand Canyon a national monument. Thanks to John Muir, people can still visit these beautiful places today.

VOTES FOR WOMEN

Despite the progress reformers made on behalf of children, the poor, and even nature, women still did not have *suffrage*, or the right to vote. By 1913, women had been working for suffrage for over fifty years. A woman named Alice Paul decided it was time woman's suffrage got some attention. On the day before Woodrow Wilson became president, Alice organized a suffrage parade. Eight thousand women and men were led down Pennsylvania Avenue by a woman on a white horse. Many people in Washington, D.C., came to watch. When Woodrow Wilson arrived at the train station, there were no crowds to greet him. "Where are the people?" he asked. "Watching the suffrage parade," was the reply.

PICKETING AT THE WHITE HOUSE
Women *picketed*, or marched, in front of the White House with banners and signs demanding their rights. Other women handed out pamphlets that explained why they should be allowed to vote.

Official Program WOMAN SUFFRAGE Procession

Washington D.C. March 3, 1913

The colors of the suffrage movement were purple, gold, and white.

MR. PRESIDENT HOW LONG MUST WOMEN WAIT FOR LIBERTY

U of M

DANGER!
Woman's Suffrage Would Double the Irresponsible Vote

It is a MENACE to the Home, Men's Employment and to All Business

I WISH MA COULD VOTE

JEERING
Crowds often jeered when women marched for their voting rights. "Stay at home where you belong!" people shouted at them. "Where are your skirts?" they mocked the men marchers.

NO VOTES FOR WOMEN
Many people, including some women, did not want women to have the right to vote. They didn't think it was ladylike for women to speak their minds.

VOTES FOR WOMEN

Despite the progress reformers made on behalf of children, the poor, and even nature, women still did not have *suffrage*, or the right to vote. By 1913, women had been working for suffrage for over fifty years. A woman named Alice Paul decided it was time woman's suffrage got some attention. On the day before Woodrow Wilson became president, Alice organized a suffrage parade. Eight thousand women and men were led down Pennsylvania Avenue by a woman on a white horse. Many people in Washington, D.C., came to watch. When Woodrow Wilson arrived at the train station, there were no crowds to greet him. "Where are the people?" he asked. "Watching the suffrage parade," was the reply.

PICKETING AT THE WHITE HOUSE
Women *picketed*, or marched, in front of the White House with banners and signs demanding their rights. Other women handed out pamphlets that explained why they should be allowed to vote.

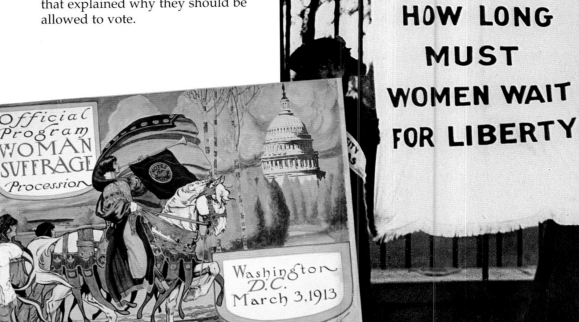

Official Program WOMAN SUFFRAGE Procession

Washington D.C. March 3, 1913

The colors of the suffrage movement were purple, gold, and white.

MR. PRESIDENT HOW LONG MUST WOMEN WAIT FOR LIBERTY

DANGER!
Woman's Suffrage Would Double the Irresponsible Vote
It is a MENACE to the Home, Men's Employment and to All Business

I WISH MA COULD VOTE

JEERING
Crowds often jeered when women marched for their voting rights. "Stay at home where you belong!" people shouted at them. "Where are your skirts?" they mocked the men marchers.

NO VOTES FOR WOMEN
Many people, including some women, did not want women to have the right to vote. They didn't think it was ladylike for women to speak their minds.

MR. PRESIDENT WHAT WILL YOU DO FOR WOMAN SUFFRAGE

JAILED FOR FREEDOM
Alice Paul was arrested seven times for picketing the White House. After women won the right to vote, she designed the Jailed for Freedom pin and gave it to the many suffragists who had served prison sentences.

Buttons helped spread the message.

WOMEN SHOULD VOTE

WE WANT TO VOTE FOR PRESIDENT

VOTES FOR WOMEN

WOMEN GET THE VOTE!
On August 26, 1920, women officially won the right to vote. Now women could help choose their government officials—something white American men had been doing for almost 150 years.

A Peek into the Future

From the book *Samantha Learns a Lesson*

"I believe Americans want to be good. I believe we want to be kind. And if we are kind, I believe we will take care of the children. Then we can truly be proud of our factories and our progress."

—Samantha Learns a Lesson

In 1904, when Samantha Parkington was just nine years old, she stood onstage at the Mount Bedford Opera House and told the audience what she believed to be true. If machines could hurt the children who worked inside factories, then America was not making good progress.

Samantha wanted to make a difference in her changing world. As she grew older, what might her life have been like? Perhaps in 1911, as a young lady of 16, she would have been shocked and saddened by the deaths of factory girls and women in the Triangle Shirtwaist Factory fire in New York City. Like many reformers, she might have given speeches demanding safer working conditions in all factories.

Alice Windsor Hunt was a reformer during Samantha's time. She worked hard to make people aware of the dangerous working conditions and low wages in factories. "I have no time to worry about the past," she said once. "I'm too busy trying to improve the present."

And the future, Samantha might have added. In 1913, she and Aunt Cornelia might have marched with thousands of other suffragists in the Woman's Suffrage Parade in Washington, D.C. Samantha would be 25 years old before Congress passed the law giving women voting rights. In 1920, Samantha could have gone to the polling booth and proudly cast her first vote. Maybe she would have even driven to the polling booth in her own Model-T automobile!